Home.

By: Morsus Engel

Home
Originally Published in the United States
Cover Design by Morsus Engel
ISBN: 978-1-365-28056-6

Table of Contents

Preface.

I've always found it strange how we heal. Piece by piece, moment by moment, never truly grasping that our body is fixing us up from the inside out as we merely breathe. I began this book more than a year ago, and the poems within date back to 2012. When I finished this book last year, my words were sloppy and many of my poems did not even make it into the book due to their graphic nature. At that point of my life, I was young, heartbroken and could pound out many angst ridden poems in under an hour. I wanted to release the book, but as I read through it, I didn't feel satisfied. As if the book had no real purpose but to be an unfinished memoir of a lonely teenage girl.

July 2016 rolled around and I wrote a poem called "18" that served as an epiphany for the creation of this book. While writing it, I realized that after many years of my heartbroken musings, I'd finally found a way to just *be okay*. It was then that I realized that I had healed. Poem by poem, word by word, I found myself, and I found *home* within myself.

A great deal of healing relies on you finding your home. Growing up, I placed home in the arms of people who were not me, places that were not mine and fantasies of perfection. For me, home did not exist. This book contains nearly everything. Not just the poems about healing, but the poems about heartbreak, romantic love, self-love and human observation. Each pertaining to some aspect of the process of finding home.

I encourage you to also consider where your home lies. Whether you have one or you are still searching, I hope your home is someplace beautiful.

1. Love.

When I began my adventure into poetry and prose, many of my works revolved around other people and the love I had for them. I was in my mid-teens, placing my home and my heart in the hands of people I saw as lovers. To me, being loved was a form of validation and as long as someone loved me, I had someplace to call home with them.

So here is the first chapter of my book, all about loving and being loved.

This is who i was, not who i am,
I hated love and the idea of
it. Yet I craved. I craved
for it as my sole means of
self-love. This was not a
reality. Reality and the
beauty of hind-sight has
taught me it was not a
means for self love, rather
that of self-harm.

Wednesday.

pretty things.
like snow,
softer than rosebud lips
dipped in cherry red
sin.
dirty things.
like a bed,
two bodies tangled in sheets,
gritty coffee grounds
and a romance
that never sleeps.

Nudity.

Sometimes, you just want to see someone completely naked.
And by naked, I mean stripped of all inhibitions, all of their barriers
torn down.
You just want to see them laugh as if dandelions were tickling their toes,
smile as if they've been kissed by the sky.
You want to see them cry when they've broken,
yell when they're enraged.
You want to see their deepest hidden emotions, their greatest passions.
You want to know that they're like you; Naked inside.

But, what if one can't deal
with nakedness?
What if I am so crazy,
so deeply broken that
I am never naked.
Not even to myself.
I hide;
behind lies,
behind walls,
behind clothes,
I hide from mirrors,
Instead I use cameras,
falsefying myself,
creating an image to hide behind.
I am scared of my truth.
Of my own reality.
So i continue to hide behind
a representation
a re interpretation,
one that is better,
that is easier to bare.

But what happens when the
camera breaks?

7

Free.

he reminds me of linens drying in the wind
almost about to break free
almost.
and that feeling of tilting your neck back,
exposing your vulnerable self to the heavens.
that's him.
he's every poem i ever read when i was fourteen, begging a universe for a
second chance.
comforting, cruel, abrupt and life changing.
i said i love you to him once,
he laughed,
such a pretty laugh that i forgot
he was laughing in the first place.
it sounded like the creek i grew up next to,
tinkling, unrestrained and gentle.
more than anything, he wanted to be liberated,
unburdened,
unaware of his own insignificance.
it was a foolish concept,
but i think the idea freed him.
so sometimes i daydream, pretending that
we are in love.
i pretend that i am his liberation
and that he loves me as much
as he loves being free.
but he continues to chase the sky,
tripping and stumbling along the way,
never losing sight of everything above him,
and i keep a watchful eye,
because something that rare,
deserves to exist.
he never belonged to anyone.
not even to himself.
he's quite the simple thing.
and i am in love with the way
he reminds me of how the
good days felt.

Soulmates: Love at First Sight.

I've always believed in love at first sight.

Yet I don't believe that a mere glance at another human's appearance or physique is a sufficient way to inspire love.

Instead, I believe that the moment you catch a glimpse of someone's soul, you are completely capable of falling in love with it.

Two souls searching for each other, finally noticing their companion hidden inside a human body.

That's the kind of love at first sight I believe in.

I agree.

However, when can that moment be defined.
When they cry? when they want to die?
What about when they laugh?
What happens then.

On Love.

Love isn't as beautiful as we make it seem.

Love isn't always about waking up to your lover's soft skin and gentle eyes, sometimes it's about waking up to their rank breath, and pushing them off to brush their teeth before fucking them while your moans spill out the windows.

Love isn't always about lavish dinners every night with roses to decorate, sometimes it's about the nights you spend in front of the TV eating take-out Chinese in your sweats.

Love isn't always about falling in love while you are hand in hand, watching the sun dip into the earth, sometimes it's about falling in love while you're staying in a beat up motel on a road trip to nowhere.

Love isn't always about spectacular dates in the city, joined with fondue and Louis Vuitton, sometimes it's about dates in those bouncy houses and trampoline arenas you cherished as children.

Love isn't simply a feeling, it is an experience.

Love isn't just about the cliché romantic moments straight out of a Nicholas Sparks novel.

Love is also about the moments that you are completely at ease with your lover.

Once you are able to expose the most vulnerable parts of you, the ones that make you human, and accept each other regardless, that is love.

Because love is utterly human. It isn't all about strawberries coated in chocolate fondue or the starry skies. It's about the little human things we don't hand to anybody else.

And we wouldn't have it any other way.

These vulnerable parts you speak of.

What if, in actuality, it is these that make us Inhuman.

"You fell in love with a crazy person"
Really?

What if there are too many vulnerable parts
Does this make the potential to love and be loved

10   Obsolete.

Vulnerable.
She's scary beautiful.
She speaks in riddles that set fire to every part of my body.
She touches me in ways that bring earthquakes to my already fluttering
heart.
She catches my eye and electricity ruptures my weakening mind.
She's destroying me,
she's a natural disaster and I've become so vulnerable to her.
But fuck it. I love her.

"I found you all by myself"

Sex.

Let us not fuck tonight,
Let us make art through sex
I want to drag masterpieces through your back, nails like paintbrushes
that haven't seen a canvas in decades.
I want you to leave me with hickeys dipped in indigo and deep rose.
I want our breaths, our moans and our words to spiral together into
song, music that drips from our lips and makes love to our ears.
I want you to track my eyes for a moment, remind me that it's only us in
this moment, only us. Art is created from the deepest parts of our souls,
and that is what I want our sex to be.
Art.

Here You Begin.

I don't want to write you poetry.
When I write you poetry,
you become something to me.
When I write the way you exist,
I have to admit that you mean something to me.
I can't write you poetry.
When I write you poetry,
I become vulnerable to your every deed.
When I write you poetry,
I won't stop writing you poetry.
When I write you poetry,
I'll have a stack of poems all addressed to you and nowhere to put them.
I don't want to write you poetry.

Let me deny your place in my heart a little longer,
please.
Oh.
I think this is almost poetry.

Fuck.
So here is where you begin.

The Type of Girl.

She's the type of girl who cries when she's happy because goddamn, it's sad that happiness surprises her this much. → How I feel when I look at her.

She's the type of girl who wanders the deepest forests armed with an itty bitty flashlight and a desire to get more lost in trees than she does in her own life.

She's the type of girl who will start fights with you at 3 in the morning when your lights are turned down so low you can barely see the thoughts whirling behind your half shut eyelids.

She's the type of girl who leans in so close just to get a look into your eyes, that you smell yourself on her lips.

She's the type of girl who romanticizes adventures across the country, yet still comes home every night to fall asleep in your arms.

She's the type of girl who wants everyone to know that she's alive, because then maybe she'll start to feel alive herself.

She's the type of girl who won't drink coffee because of the paranoia that arrives for dessert. She's learned other ways to keep herself up at night.

She's the type of girl who writes love songs about nobody in particular, because love songs sound so much different when there's no history attached.

She's the type of girl who doesn't need anyone to help fix her, she has a first aid kit filled with all of her healing music and the most passionate poetry ever written to put her back together.

She's the type of girl who loves the same things that other people in the world do, but you'll still find her unique.

She's the type of girl to fall asleep on beds in furniture stores, dreaming about a day when her life could feel as peaceful as that.

She's the type of girl who writes about herself in rambling poetry, trying to figure herself out as she jots down the things she feels set her apart.

She's the type of girl someone's going to fall in love with, maybe it'll be you.

She's the type of woman to cherish.

Because she's the type of girl who'll cherish you too.

14

Musings.

Let's talk about sex, your conspiracy theories and the beauty of death.
Let's bathe there, in some vast woody corner, and have no clue what
we're trying to say.
Let's talk until our tongues flap in the wind pouring meaningless words
into the air.
I like the way your lips move. I like the way your voice sounds. Let's talk
about nothing.
Let's fall in love.

Jade –

5am – moral absolutism.

Innocent.

i remember you peeled your shoes off and tossed them behind you,
barefoot, running through the scalding sand with arms outstretched to
greet the wind.
you threw your head back in delight and spun a quick twirl, teetering
back and forth on your toes.
you beckoned me then, the wildest, the most liberated grin stretching
across your face.
your curls hung soft and pretty over your dark eyelashes, your t shirt sat
lopsided over your shoulders, and you,
you were dancing in the sand, trying your hardest not to get burned.
i chuckled at you, i told you to go out and run your fingers through the
ocean, dip your feet in, make the edge of the earth your own.
and so you did.
and all i could do was watch from afar.
smiling to myself,
wondering how on earth i was so lucky to get a chance to love you.

10 Ways to Love Her.

Keep this in mind:

1. She hates her stretch marks, she thinks they're ugly, and that's why she'll flinch whenever your eyes graze down her body.

2. She doesn't think she deserves affection, so she'll minimize her own beauty.

3. Not only does she minimize her beauty, she doesn't really believe in it. So tell her that she's beautiful. Mean it too.

4. She desires you, her whole body and mind craves you. But sometimes she's afraid to get attached. So she'll push you away. Fight for her anyways.

5. She's going to want to make you feel special, let her. Let her do things for you.

6. Sometimes she'll say no. Accept that.

7. She's not all that happy. And no, you don't have to fix her. You can't. You just have to show her that she matters. She can fix herself.

8. Show her the stars, show her the sunset, show her the sky. She'll find peace when she looks into an infinity.

9. Tell her everyday how much you love her. She loves you too, and she loves hearing you do.

10. Open up to her. She needs to feel that you're there for her, all of you. She's never liked secrets.

Things He Said to Me, pt.1

You're beautiful.

I love seeing your eyes turn hazel in the sunlight, I love watching your hair float in the wind.

I love the simple things about you, like the way you drape your arm out the window to feel the 60 mph winds making love to your fingers.

I can tell, you love to see the world move fast, you love to fly, you never sit still, always anticipating your next escape.

I love seeing you happy, it feels like sunny mornings and syrupy waffles.

You kiss like a madwoman but you talk like a scholar.

I could live all my life with your hands around my waist, with you, I forget everything I had meant to forget,

and damn, it's beautiful.

Sinking.

and so I asked,
"what's the best way to fall in love?"
and he chuckled as if he knew all along that I'd be asking about this
someday.
his eyes met mine just a second before he spoke.
he said,
"the best way to fall in love,
is not to fall,
but sink,
sink into love.
sink the way you would into a rich, chocolate cake,
let it engulf you, consume you, swallow you whole.
sink into it until it's all you feel, sink until your knees give out and your
body arches upwards.
falling in love, now that's just too sudden, too quick, you never get a
moment to feel it all,
everything.
but when you sink into love,
you feel,
more than you ever wanted to,
but you truly, genuinely, passionately feel,
and that's the best way to exist in love."

The Photograph.

And for a second,
it looked like they were in love.
So I captured it, I
took a photo so blurry, so fuzzy
that not much could be seen.
But the two of them,
that's all anyone needed to see.
I took it, so that if one day
they ever denied being in love,
I could pull that photo from
the depths,
and perhaps
they too would realize,
that even if just for a second,
they were in love,
and unbearably so.

Vibe to the Rhythm of Me.

Vibe baby, vibe.

You don't need music for your body to come alive.

Let me take you by the tongue and show you the soul that exists inside.

Rip away your indecision and misunderstandings.

Fuck your inhibitions, because baby look, your legs are dancing.

Vibe baby, vibe.

Hear the way my lips make your gut scream in a hunger for more.

Feel the way my fingers feed your nerves and pull you to the floor.

Your heart races. It races right out of your chest and straight into mine.

You're collapsing into me, losing yourself in me, and you're telling me it's fine.

Vibe baby, vibe.

Let me speak into your ear, let you hear the way I feed off your love.

Your legs might quiver, you'll barely breathe, calling me an angel from above.

You'll realize that we feel the same, we've become the same, we are a unison choir.

And so you'll hand me yourself, in exchange for myself, nearly lost in our desires.

Vibe baby, vibe.

You don't need music for your body to come alive.

Natural Disaster.

Earthquake.
You and I,
We are
An earthquake.
Your fingers dipped into the fault lines
Of my arching spine.
My lips locked
On the shaky ground
Of your heartbeat.
There is tender skin
Between your fingers.
It is the gentlest part of
The connection
Between
You and I.
The walls close in.
The photos slip from their
Nails.
Your eyes gape wide
When you see how our
Hips collide.
The wind,
That rushes from your exhale,
whisks the papers
Off my desk.
Your hands pulse softly
And stir up shivers
Along the curves of my spine.
We're on the brink of an
Aftershock.
So when the windows burst open
And we watch as the contents
Of this room
Spill outside,
We will twist together
And see
If we can bring it all back
With just one
More time.

When we are done,
Everything will be broken.
Yet the bond
Between us
Will have never been this
Strong.
And you'll tell me
That it looks like
A disaster.
And I'll tell you
That we are an earthquake
And we are a mess
Together
We have survived.

Jade

Yes, we are a mess.
It is sticky, like chewing gum

We could survive
We would survive.

But don't you swallow your
chewing gum?

Darling.

I could tell you stories about how the stars fell just as fast as we did.
Or about how we found hope in each other when we felt hopeless.
Or about the dreams I have every night, your essence coming alive
through my slumber.
I could tell you that you make me smile in ways I forgot I could.
But all I'll tell you, is that I love you.
The rest is implied.

Jade,

you must know,
you must know that is
what I mean,
when i say i love you,

I speak of
Jane + TL,
I speak of Wagamamas,
I speak of my springless bed
of the dirty sheets and even
dirtier secrets,
of the cold cups of tea
and your warm breath
condensing on my shoulder.

This all means,
I Love You
- A

Critique of a Cliché.

Poets love to tell you that you will never be able to love anybody
until you love yourself,
and that nobody can *really* love you
until you love yourself.
I would like to challenge this cliché.

I can tell you that my mother has loved me since the day I was born,
when I did not know how to feel love,
to this very day, when I am still learning to love myself.
She forces her fingers into my gut every night,
searching for the self-love I swallowed around the age of thirteen.
And if that isn't love, I don't know what is.
And I know that no matter how little or how much I love myself,
my mother will always love me more.
Because though you may not love yourself,
people who love you will be a part of your journey to self-love.

Now to the notion that you cannot love another
until you love yourself.
It is always easier to love others than yourself.
We crave to see the best in those we love,
but so quickly find the worst in ourselves.
The reason I know that I do not completely love myself
is because I have loved others so dearly,
and what I feel for myself, does not feel like that.
I know what love is.
And just because I am incapable of pouring my own love
down my throat,
does not mean that I won't pour it down the throat of someone
who makes my skin feel like *home*.

Sex and Adventure.

Call it divine, those old motels dusty from reckless customers of years past. Our new love blossoming under a rag of a blanket, blotchy crimson, stained by a healthy dose of vomit and who knows what else.

Call it sacred, an afternoon call strained by bad connection and a need to hear a voice, any voice. Our conversation held a needle and thread to my stomach, stitching my insides up by the aid of your college boy croon.

Call it enlightening, an appointment in Pearl District, dotted with upper class folk clamoring in their stilettos, hobbling to the nearest cafe. Our hands intertwined were outsiders to this arena, cautiously reminding the world that wealth is paid for by a degree of loneliness.

Call it holy, a just sprung park in the spring, far from intimidating city lights yet drenched in the light of stars. Our souls came together in empty space, gasping for breath and a chance to connect with something fuller than life itself.

Call it spiritual, a barred up basement room deprived of light, simply torn up carpet and the smell of mildew. Our heads were not visible, but your fingers throbbed with curiosity and cautious desire everywhere they brushed, painting colors not even I could define.

Call it what you want, two bodies, two souls, two hearts, bare in the arms of each other, quietly infatuated with a dream of forever. Our time was short, yet so well lived, nothing I could ever regret, everything my heart exists to embrace.

Call it love.

Oh please, call it love.

Boy, I'm Gonna Love You.

We're on the brink of another 'I love you.'

At least I am.

This wouldn't be the first time I've filled my organs with cheap perfume, hoping that the lonely scent of empty alleyways and chewed up pencils would have the capability to be alluring.

I like to pretend that I'm something rare, a star, illuminating herself so bright that she sometimes forgets to see.

I do forget to see, I forget to see that I am not a star so bright like that at all.

I forget to see because I don't want to see.

I'm simply the star that shoots across the sky for a second, to vanish before your eyes.

~ I'm the star that is wished upon, not the one who is wished for. ~

They call my situation denial, I know denial all too well.

Denial runs in my bones, just as thick as the cheap perfume.

Denial is the way I write poems about love when the love I knew only existed in poems.

Denial is the way that I always rush in a few seconds late, so that if I miss anything, I can blame the situation instead of myself.

Denial is bittersweet.

Denial tastes a hell of a lot like the time he said 'goodbye,' and how I erased that message and never replied.

But I like you. I like the way you appear in my head. I like the way you dance on paper, the way you make the ink your own.

I like the way you sound when I replay your voice in your head. You're a little different than the last boy I could've loved. But I'll have to warn you;

My love is not going to be anything like the movies. And if you choose to let me go, I promise you, the smell of cheap perfume will hide in your sheets for years.

The Tiger and The Sphinx.

You were a boy who knew how to send shivers up my spine with one mere touch. You had a perpetual supply of heat, and your passion for me was everlasting.

He was a man who knew how to make love to my ears before he ever set one finger on me, and he had a warming presence, one that was more pleasant than terrifying.

But I couldn't pick either of you. Because though you knew how to love me, sometimes I simply wanted a night in with cups of tea and just your arms around me.
Neither of you knew how to give me that.

Things He Said to Me pt. 2.

But baby girl, 10 years from now you'll be cruising down I-5 with the sunset falling behind you like velvet drapes and it'll be the beginning of something profound. Let me go, so that you can build yourself up to that very second. Let me go, so that when you throw your hands up to the sky, your fingers will be free to shake hands with tomorrow.

And baby girl, I love you. I'll crash with the velvet drape sunsets and let you roam free with the stars. All I want is for you to breathe oxygen that smells like first rain.

Now, baby girl, it's time for you to let me go. I promise, you'll discover a different brand of joy to wear.
Just call me when you do because I want to be the one to tell you;
'I told you so, baby girl.

Jade,
what if I don't want to
what if I don't want to let you go.

Do Not Push Me Away.

My love is not your decision.

Skin, Skin, Skin.

I like the feeling of skin on skin,
of bodies pressed into each other as if stamping a brand of vitality onto
the others stomach.
I rather enjoy simple things, stripped of all decoration,
the way a body becomes poetry in the eyes of a lover, filling them up
with a sense of admiration that escapes through their lips.
I appreciate a good taste of vulnerability on occasion,
how souls come out to make love for the first time, escaping bodies for a
second of acknowledgement and sacrifice.
I desire the moments after and the moments before,
when words run into each other and seep into memories, collectively
birthing a feeling of euphoria. Everything's golden then.
I crave nostalgia like a weary old lover,
thinking about strange bodies becoming one body, watching a maroon
sun melt into an ocean, feeling a tender hand caressing more than just
your fingers.
I visit my lover often,
his words still drip off his lips like a leaky faucet, one I've yet to turn off.
He only lives in the back of my mind now, I chose to keep him preserved
before his words ran out.
I quite generously exist in intimacy,
with words like aphrodisiacs and lips like temptation, still knowing that
fingers intertwining is the most intimate act of them all.
I need to feel,
like wordy poetry mustering up enough emotion to dump onto the very
last line.
Like mustering up enough emotion to write wordy poetry on how much
I still feel your skin grazing mine on lazy Friday afternoons.
I love the feeling of skin on skin,
of bodies collapsing at 4 am, piling on each other in sloppy heaves and
messy grins, then understanding that every moment was nothing more
than a chance to exist.

Goodnight.

I said "I love you"
You smiled and said goodnight
You needed to hear it
To know
That you were worth something
You loved seeing me
Tripping over your broken pieces
and falling for you.

I did love you.
When you smiled and said goodnight
I wanted to hear it too
To know
That I meant something
That you loved seeing me.
While I was picking up your pieces
maybe you were falling for me too.
"Goodnight"

For Him.

It's not that you haven't been designed for love,
and it's not that love hasn't been designed for you.
It's just that you haven't yet learned how to be gentle with hearts,
and you've been designed to learn, you see?
You've been designed to hurt, and break, and stumble until you finally
learn just how you love.
You have been designed human, seeking love in strange places.
And when you finally learn how to make those strange places look like
home,
then you will know that you were
always
designed to learn love.

Maroon Love. — *Our love is maroon. Inside out.*

Love looks beautiful in the color
maroon.
Consuming, abundant and thrilling.
Imagine bathing in maroon.
Engulfing your eyelids, pulling your lips apart, seeping into the naked
parts of your body.
Yet,
maroon feels quite sad too.
Imagine peeling the pages back of a book stained maroon.
Words that have become unreadable, like a code you were never meant
to decipher.
Your fingers staining a maroon that a thousand washes will never rinse
out.
Imagine a world tainted maroon,
the deep kind of red we see in blood.
Doesn't it seem sinister?
Maroon love is the most beautiful to look at,
the prettiest of stories,
the epitome of desire.
Yet maroon love terrifies me.
Love in maroon lacks the calm of blue, lacks the delight of yellow, lacks
the childlike wonder of pink.
Maroon love is fiery,
so fiery that you can't help but get
burned.

2. Loss.

The scariest thing about creating a home in other people, is that once they leave, you have no home. For a long few years of my life I was heartbroken, searching for a home when those I had loved left.

So, many poems were written, me trying to find something worthwhile beneath the madness.

Welcome to the second chapter of my book, all about the darker side to love and loss.

The Same.

And if you leave,
stay gone.
I forgive too easily,
and I'm afraid that I'll take you back
with open arms.

I've said goodbye,
I told you that I could never forgive you.
I told you that you had lost me.
But that's one thing we have in common,
sometimes we both lie to keep our problems
away.

Lies.

A bookshelf I cleared of all your letters to me, little angel figurines
dusting over and dried flowers from your garden.
I told myself you'd come back someday.

A gym bag shaken to empty out its contents, the smell of your cologne
wafting past my lips and straight onto my neck.
I told myself you'd come back someday.

Pictures, messages, knick-knacks and memories falling to pieces at the
stroke of my thumb, all things that remind me of you.
I told myself you'd come back someday.

Seeing you walk to her with a beaming grin plastered on your face and
feeling the earth vibrate to shake me out of my senses.
I told myself you'd come back someday.

Hearing you tell your friends that she defined your perception of true
love, while I curled up on a shelf with dust and spiders for friends.
I told myself you'd come back someday.

Pen marks that stained my sheets with your name, the same name I try
every day not to let slip my lips.
I told myself you'd come back someday.

Turning my cheek until reality slapped me across that same cheek to
remind me that you live on both sides of me.
I told myself you'd come back someday.

Trying for months to explain the way I felt, but always falling short of
describing the knots, twists and tangles you perpetually danced on.
I told myself you'd come back someday.

And now I'm writing some mediocre poetry about you, for readers who
are hoping I stopped telling myself you'd come back someday.
I tell myself you'll come back someday.

Fading.

You're the reason I've grown afraid.
Of goodbyes, hellos and things that fade.
You're the reason I stitch my lips shut.
It keeps me from starting things I won't finish up.

Lo(v/s)ing Her.

And when it was all done and over,
he said that
he only ever regretted things that were within his control,
and that he could never regret loving her.
Because
loving her was well out of his control,
no matter what,
no matter when,
he would've loved her sometime.
He was just lucky she came around so early in his life.
And if he was given another chance,
a chance to love someone that wasn't her,
he said he'd still love her,
time and time again,
even if it broke his heart
every damn time.

The Voicemail.

"The person you are trying to reach is not available right now, please leave a message after the tone."

-beep-

Hey? Sorry it's been such a long time since I've called, I've been busy and I know you have been too. I found some of your old voicemails, man those brought back some memories. They're just sitting there, and I just thought maybe I should call, let you know that I'm doing okay. I hope you're okay, I've been seeing your tweets and all, looks like you're doing fine. Congratulations on getting into NYU! I knew that you could do it, you've always been so intelligent. Congratulations on your new girlfriend too, you guys are so beautiful together.

I know it's been two years. But remember when you used to call me every morning? I miss that, you were always so easy to talk to. So many memories with you, and they still hurt a little. Like that last message you sent me, telling me that you were too busy to talk, even though I could see full well that you were with that other girl. Gosh she was lovely, so gorgeous.

Wow I've been rambling and I'm so sorry! I just want to catch up with you. I want to hear your voice again you know? It's been so long. The last time we talked, your grandpa had just passed. I'm sorry about that, I hope you're doing fine. Thank you for those great memories, I wrote a lot of poetry about the way we ended things. So much frothing, furious poetry. Seriously, you really inspired my creative juices to make a comeback. But that's not the point anyways.

I miss you,

And I think I still lov-

-beep-

Ugly Boy.

pretty boy.
pretty boy loved me.
pretty boy thought i was pretty too.
pretty boy touched my wrist
left pretty bruises on pretty skin.
pretty boy loved me.
pretty boy called me his.
so i was pretty boy's.
pretty boy bellowed my pretty name
right into my pretty ear.
it didn't sound too pretty.
but pretty boy loved me.
pretty boy loved me.
pretty boy liked to throw things around.
pretty boy liked to throw me around.
pretty boy said i was his.
pretty boy called me names
honey, baby, sweetheart, whore.
almost pretty names.
pretty boy loved me.
pretty boy loved me.
i didn't want pretty boy to turn ugly boy.
i wanted pretty boy to stay pretty boy.
because pretty boy loved me.
i loved pretty boy.

Yours.

the day i left you
was the day i fell apart.
i hated it, i hated seeing you
pretend like you weren't on the verge of
tears.
i hated pretending not to notice.
but i needed it.
i couldn't get you out of my mind
so i chose to leave my mind behind.
i let you have it, i let you live in it.
leaving pieces of me behind was the only way
i knew how to get away from you.
and i thought that it would work. i really did.
tragically, it didn't.
because as you can see, my body still knows you
my gentle hands continue to write all about you.
i handed you all of me, everything.
i'm still yours and
i don't want to be.

I Don't Want to Feel You.

kiss me a goodbye,
forget me at hello.
let me go before i make you *home*.
be a monstrosity for me,
be a bitter berry for me.
run before i miss you
get away before i notice you've been around.

Letting Her Go.

Let her go and someday you'll see her in the lulls of traffic where she'd always stick her head out the window to feel the breeze tugging at strands of her hair.

Let her go and someday you'll see her in strange women with different names, her poise blanketed over one woman, her lips plopped onto another, pieces that don't seem to fit on anyone but her.

Let her go and someday you'll hear her favorite song on some radio station somewhere and your heart won't beat for a while. You'll feel your body moving to the rhythm of her absent little head bobs and foot taps.

Let her go and someday you'll have to begin the process of forgetting. You'll scroll through numerous photographs and rummage through an accumulation of her stuff, now your stuff, while her scent lazily floats off to wedge doorstops into every door you need to shut.

Let her go and someday you'll cross paths with her favorite places, maybe by accident, maybe on purpose. Bridges back to her soul will begin to rebuild themselves as you take in the indigo sky and remember everything you meant to forget.

Let her go and someday you'll see her, really her, passing through a small section of the mall. She'll be happier than ever with a look of utter joy pulling at her lips, pulling her so far away from you that she begins to look like an illusion.

Let her go and someday you'll realize that you never truly can let her go at all.

Feeling.

sometimes I get so angry
with myself
for allowing my feelings to fester up,
grow like twisted vines.
because I swore I'd be independent,
swore I'd keep away from temptation,
but here I am,
once more,
dabbling in the art of
feeling
just a little too much.

Missed Connections.

It was 4:30 pm, you were rushing through the crowded streets, coffee cup in hand, trying to spot a taxi to carry you off to the airport.
You crashed into someone and spilled your coffee all over their shirt.
You let out a slew of curse words and hoped that this person wasn't as angry as they could've been.
Surprisingly, they weren't.
You caught their eye as they smiled at you for a split second.
"Say, you seem awfully busy today, don't you?"
You let out a small chuckle, nodded your head, apologized, and told them you were running late.
And as anyone else would do, they let you go.
So you scurried off to meet a taxi cab in the swell of traffic.
You never heard from that stranger again.
Maybe you were supposed to forget your responsibilities for a second.
Maybe you were supposed to hold a conversation with that stranger just a little longer.
But if something was supposed to happen between the two of you,
you will never know.

Hundreds of missed connections a day.
It's almost insignificant.
and,
I know that heartbreak is sad. When an overwhelming love has to come to an end,
it's tragic.
But there's something just as tragic about a love that never has the chance to begin.

The Morning After.

The morning after tastes like dark chocolate, leaving a sticky residue on your tongue, subtly sweet with a bitter bite to fill your throat.

The morning after is when you pick up pillows from the floor and stack them up nice and neat. You'll make sure to keep them next to you before you sleep, just to feel something close at night.

The morning after is when you pick up your phone to check for missed calls and angry text messages. This is the heaviest empty inbox you've ever held.

The morning after feels like Velcro, gripping onto you with itchy pieces of fabric, pulling at your skin, reminding you that it'll find a way beneath even your toughest armor.

The morning after is when you brush my teeth and stare at your reflection in the mirror. Swollen lips and empty eye bags gaze back. You'll brush for ten minutes thinking about how clean your teeth need to be, how clean your teeth need to be, how clean your teeth need to be, need to be.

The morning after is when you forget to eat breakfast, because there's no reason for you to fill a stomach that's just going to feel empty for the rest of the day anyway.

The morning after speaks in a riddle you'll never find the heart to decipher. There's no willpower left in you to do anything but breathe.

The morning after is when you'll sleep for half the day, knowing that your dreams won't feel as numbing as the room you've holed yourself up in.

The morning after is when all the breakup songs you paid no heed to on your playlist will suddenly hit every nerve, breaking your heart on the tumble down.

The morning after is when you'll realize that it's all just over now. You've made it to the after. Nothing comes after The After.

The morning after is when the real heartbreak happens. Loneliness and confusion pluck hope right out of your ribs and fly off to bully you until you fight back again.

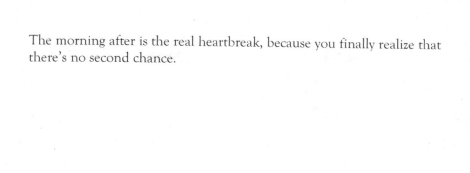

The morning after is the real heartbreak, because you finally realize that there's no second chance.

Note: It gets better. It does.

Deadly Poison.

I suppose our hearts are more poisonous than our minds.
We can lose our minds, but save fragments of our minds within our hearts.
Yet when our heart breaks,
we lose our minds.

Part Two.

And I'm in love with him again.

I saw him in the jagged cliffs of rocks against the ocean, the way he quickly broke everything coming his way.

And I saw him in the acres of sky, the way he was ever changing, but always his rawest at sunset when his messages became flustered and passionate.

And I heard him in the pluck of guitar strings, the way he made music so easily when placed in the right hands.

And I felt him inside the warm arches of my heart, the way he somehow got trapped within, and never found a way out.

So that's why I'm still in love with him.

Because I can't escape him.

And he hasn't escaped me.

A Quick Fuck.

i feel
ripples
skin like
still water
fingers,
fingers everywhere
fingers making love
to my hair
fingers clutching
skin
for dear life
breaths
breaths easing me
to arch myself
to greet the body
above me
lips
lips like pillows
lulling me into a dream
keeping me in a fantasy
sounds,
unfiltered sounds,
raw sounds,
naked sounds
i feel teeth
teeth grazing skin
sparking goosebumps
electric
electric
sparks,
no,
fire,
no,
lightning,
no,
fireworks,
no,

i feel skin
skin like cotton
skin like comfort
skin like love,
no,
lust
i see eyes
vulnerable eyes
eyes lost in a moment
forgetting to be cold
breaths
breaths
breaths that sound like
confessions,
like sin,
like falling in love
with what was meant
to be a
quick fuck.

Love, The Miracle Drug.

Love can be easily compared to a drug,
and it's been done,
many times.
And with every drug comes side effects.
Now, often I am asked why I don't just face up and take the drug of love
to cure the awful disease of loneliness.
Is it because I'm afraid of love?
To that question, I simply answer; no.
No, I am not afraid of love.
Love itself is euphoric. It's a pleasant high that leaves you full and fresh.
No, instead, I'm more concerned about the potential side effects of this
love.
Because what's written on the warning label scares me much more than
love itself.
So let us review the warning label together.

Potential side effects may include:
-Unbearable aching
-Unrequited love
-Clammy hands
-Falling for the wrong person
-Losing the right person
-Heartbreak
-Confusion
-And in some unusual cases in which love is misused, eg. Romeo and
Juliet, death.

Now that's what overwhelms me.
Love isn't so scary.
It's the side effects that I can't handle.

Berries.

Strawberry lips, raspberry tongue, blueberry eyes and blackberry soul.
You were made of berries, ones that tasted sweetest in the summer.
I kept trying to keep summer alive, but when I finally saw the pristine
snow silently covering my driveway, I realized that summer was gone.
So were you.

6 Boys That Did Not Know How to Love.

January: iced over with the promise of new beginnings. His lips comforted like woolen scarves and his words gave me chills on even the warmest nights. Every time he grasped my fingers, it felt like a new era, but deep down, I knew he had nothing but coldness inside of him. He'd seen too many beginnings to cherish them any longer.

February: gentle, sliding up behind me with maroon roses and silk boxes, telling me he loved me with every chocolate. His eyes were in a constant state of ecstasy and his heart raced a little too fast sometimes. He said he loved me, but I knew he felt nothing but lust for the woman he thought I was. He'd become so familiar with lust that he'd mistake it for love any time.

March: soft, breathing life into me, feeding me compliments and validation. He was the epitome of rebirth, and I saw myself rejuvenated whenever he bit my lip. He made me feel as if I was growing up, and I craved a taste of maturity. He allowed me to grow the way I needed to, but he did not offer much more. He never stuck around long enough to see my beauty fully bloomed, love was not his niche.

April: bright, bewildered and astonished by the very way I walked. He had a way of getting lost in every moment, telling me how spectacular it was to experience the world with me. He was forever fleeting, rushing to catch the next rainbow. His sense of adventure enamored me, but he was so focused on the things he needed to see, that he never spent much time looking at what was in front of him. He had no time to fall in love, just time to imagine it.

May: tears, always tears, tears like rainfall, anger like thunder. He poured his world on me as if unloading the heaviest of downpours. He flooded my mind with his disappointment and discontent. It was unnervingly enchanting how he was able to make everything ugly into something more beautiful, but his self-centered nature kept me from seeing past his facades. His love was hidden somewhere past his despair, but his despair never let up.

June: warm, lazy, meandering onto paths he didn't know were not his to meander onto. He was in a constant state of invitation, bringing me to his bedside day after day, just watching as the sun melted into the edge of the earth. He felt like relief from every man before him, but he was nothing more. Relaxation was his only sport, and he never wanted to pursue much else. So when the time of love came around, he deemed himself too lazy, and waited for another someone to lure to his bedside.

Just Because.

i miss you
and summer
and july
also
may 18 2014
also
falling into an abyss
that i thought looked
like love
and
i miss
calling you at 3 am
to tell you that
i forgot him
because of you
because you
loved me.
loved me.
i miss you
you taught me
a lot of things
important things.
like love
like fingers up my spine
like arching my neck back
perfectly
just so you could
learn something
about the way i looked
completely vulnerable
completely yours.
i miss that
feeling like i belonged
to something
bigger.

strange how quickly
i let myself
become something
that was not me.
strange how quickly
i let myself
miss someone
that was not mine.

The Mess.

I don't know how to say this clearly but,
Poetry begins with a hook.
Something to invite readers in, captivate them till the very end
But sometimes we can't make the filling of the poem make sense
The words spill out in jumbles, tangle themselves up in knots, writhe
and scream until the poet picks them up and does jump rope with
whatever sentences they can string together.
And I am confused now. I am not sure where I should lead this poem to
next.
The last line is what will make this poem somewhat less senseless.
Words are just dripping from the sides of my mouth now, I can't stop
writing things.
Inhale before you write. I have to inhale.
I don't want this poem to become something that it shouldn't be. I'm
avoiding spitting out what I must.
I cannot allow this poem to become just another cliché, just another
writer spilling ink that every poet has dipped their pens in.
And I'm trying so hard to decipher the ink that has spilled in front of
me, but it just looks like a blob.
Blobs are unreadable. Blobs anger me. How dare they stain such pretty
white paper with such an ugly, tar black stain.
I'm writing in knots that I do not know how to undo.
I do not know where to go with this.
I am so lost, so confused. Everything I want to say doesn't even make
sense anymore.
It sounds like the poem I wrote yesterday.
This is the dilemma of the writer, finding a purpose, finding a last line.
Some days I do not even know the last line.
Some days I do not even know if I have the strength to get there without
reliving yesterday.
I want to write that line.
I want to spit it out like a splatter of ink to taint what I have tried so
diligently to protect.
I do not know how to clearly process my thoughts.
The first line hasn't gone anywhere yet, but I need it to go to the last
line.
I need something to connect again.
I have not exhaled yet.

This is such nonsense. It's out of order, it's fucked up from the top to the bottom.

Does this poem have purpose?

Each word tells nothing more than the last, and altogether, it just looks like a truck drove by with the sole intention of hitting this piece of art and making it crumble to the ground.

Fuck you, truck.

This poem was going to be something really special until that truck fucked it up.

I let it happen though.

Mostly my fault.

But fuck you, truck.

This poem makes no sense. But I hope that you'll understand sometime.

I still love him.

My World.

I feel like my world revolves around you, like the earth revolves the sun.
And just like the earth and sun, getting too close would be disastrous.
The earth and the sun weren't meant to get too close.
Neither were we.

3. Recovery.

Regardless of how bad a heartbreak hits you, you recover. For a while you flounder, lost, unsure of anything. Yet eventually, little by little, you get better.

You may not have rebuilt your home yet, but you are rebuilding your heart. You are rebuilding yourself, and for right now, that is enough.

This chapter is dedicated to all of us who are slowly realizing that we have always only been deserving of the best.

Losing Him.

He called me a lover, walked me home every night.

Said his arms would stretch around buildings and bridges just to pull me in.

He called me at 5 am when his night terrors took over and he needed to hear a friendly voice.

My body was soothed by his existence, my ears in love with his lullaby croon.

He knew he needed me as much as I needed him, so he kept me near.

I peered up at strange city lights to feel like he was watching with me, pointing out the brightest buildings and the prettiest skyscrapers.

He told me things that made me feel impure in a sacred way.

His eyes had a large, doe look to them, so innocently placed upon a walking tragedy.

As if sending an apology note after a million bullet holes.

His favorite songs became mine as I saw his life tangled in the lyrics of his playlists, tangling myself in them to reach him.

It was gracious. It was fulfilling. It was majestic.

But tonight at 1 am, in an unfamiliar city, I long to feel his familiar touch on my unfamiliar skin.

Losing him was a romance of its own.

To Mr. X.

I cannot begin to express my frustration at all the exes who once told me
"Nobody's gonna love you more than me, nobody's gonna love you like
me."
How selfish of you to think that your love is the only love worth my
time.
How insulting it is that
you think that nobody is capable of loving me more than you did,
as if I'm not worthy of love greater than yours,
as if your love has battled thousands of battles and earned the title
"Greatest Love of All Time."
And how silly of you to think that telling me that
nobody can love me like you did
would break my heart,
would cripple me,
and make me grieve your loss
Because that's a fact we can agree on.
And we aren't together anymore for a reason.
So yeah, nobody will ever love me the way you did.
But who said I wanted your kind of love again?
Nobody will love me the way you did.
And damn, isn't that a good thing?

Small Hands.

Two hands outstretched, palms up to feel the flush of empty air.
Where your hands would have once met mine, my fingers graze raindrops.
You stopped loving me when my lips began speaking rather than simply moving.
I stopped loving you when I understood this.
My knees remain scraped from all the times I fell for you, only to find your hands reaching for mine after I'd fallen.
I got up. I'm not falling for you anymore.
The rain has washed all the dried, dark blood away.
It's so comforting to be standing on my own, balanced and free.
So comforting to have my hands outstretched in front of me, knowing that for once, you won't grab them to pull me in for another moment.

Again.

I knew that you knew what it felt like to be in love
because when I asked about your first love,
your lips quivered, you choked on your words, and you had to steady
yourself on a stop sign.
"It was-
She was-
I felt-
The, you know-
Stars and I-
I'm sorry I-
My fucking body was-
Everything-
Everything-
Just everything-
But nothing-
Fuck, April 14th just-
I can't explain it.
It just is."
Your eyes had welled over with tears, your fingers were clutching your
thigh, holding on, trying not to let go.
"But I lost her,
and that's not even the saddest part.
The saddest part is
that I'd do it again."
So I told you that I understood, helped you dry your tears, and hoped
that you'd try love again, wishing that this time, you'd try it with me.

Tripping Over Words.

When the woman asked me why I fell in love so quickly,
I told her that I had shaky legs that never found stable ground,
not even at *home*.
When she asked me why I always complained about falling in love,
I told her that I wasn't complaining about falling in love,
because that, that would always feel euphoric.
No, ma'am, I complain about the cuts, the scrapes, and the bruises that
come with falling.
Falling feels like flying for just a short second, don't you know?
And she asks how my heart does on these falls,
I let her know that my heart does well. It stays within its cage, but I've
never been able to look at it. All I know is that my skin takes most of the
damage.
When my bloodied knees catch her eye, she asks if I'd just recently
fallen.
So I tell her how I'd just tripped over some broken heart on the way
here.
I tell her how I used to stay fallen until my knees birthed new skin,
But how now, I get up before the pain hits me.
See, that's the great thing about falling in love all the time;

You learn how to get up.

Goodbye.

When their soul has faded away into plumes of smoke and your hand
clenches nothing but rotting memories,
you face a kind of death that only happens to the living.
Your body continues to work feverishly, promising that you'll be able to
walk soon,
never telling you that some days you'll refuse to get out of bed.
Some days you'll see them in the faces of strangers, and you'll muster up
a small smile as your stomach clenches up, knowing that you'll soon be
digesting the 'hello's' you swallowed back every single time.
Mostly, you'll have good days. But that won't start for a while.
There will be days where memories flood the insides of your eyelids, and
going to sleep feels like waking up to a universe where everything is still
okay.
But when you truly realize that they're gone, that they vanished, that
their hands will no longer be so warm, that their presence in your life is
nothing more than your mind making up for their absence,
I think you'll be devastated.
I know you will be.
I was.
Because the concept that holds up the word 'gone' is undefinable and
rests on my tongue like bitter medicine I defiantly refuse to swallow.
So when you realize that they're just *gone*, the medicine will sit on your
tongue until it burns.
And you'll figure out that you never really said goodbye.
You never wanted to.
Because goodbye meant *gone*.
But Goodbye never began with ends.
Goodbye always began with beginnings.
Goodbye is the start of eras.
Goodbye is the way you stop dying in their absence, and start living in
your presence.
Goodbye is the way you start to finally recover.
Goodbye is the way I wrote this poem, just to finally tell you;
Goodbye.

Making Love to a Few Moments.

we fell apart slowly,
not noticing the bits and pieces of us that flaked away
and drifted into the cotton candy clouds.
the last few months were a facade,
laughter that once gurgled out of us in uncontrollable gasps
suddenly became forced, us closing our eyes, searching for memories to
laugh over.
conversation that once exhausted us both, leaving us speechless and
enamored
became exhausting conversation, both of us without much to say,
mistaking our silence for a connection deeper than words.

you couldn't feed me i love you's anymore,
and even if you could,
i don't know how i would've stomached them.
we only stuck around so long because of habit.
good morning texts were habit,
sunday afternoon dates were habit,
10 pm phone calls were habit,
you were a habit-
like finger biting and toe tapping,
one of those ones you never have the strength to kick,
just because they aren't so fatal.

and we were in love once, that i won't deny,
but our compatibility had expired.
both of us had grown,
from each other,
ready for new things,
more things that probably wouldn't last forever.

so we fell apart slowly,
one day noticing that we were but fragments of the people we were
before,
living on a last breath.
it was then, that we took that last breath,
set each other free,
and began search for another love to make *home* in.
you say that
we may have been wasting time
precious time.
but i say that
lovers who are not meant for forever,
won't make a love less worthwhile.

Thursday Morning Muse.

I'm going to pretend that someday,
somewhere,
someplace,
I'll see you again.
Because my heart cannot bear the burden of another
"the end."
Maybe soon, I'll run into you at the greyhound station,
in a shady corner of Portland.
Maybe you'll chuckle at the way I packed too much for such a short
journey.
I always put too much into things.
You'll reminisce on my shaky legs, always running from place to place,
searching for stability.
You'll realize that I haven't changed much at all.
I'm still the girl you fell in love with at 17.
I'll always be that girl.

And then, you'll run into me again on 23rd avenue, carrying bags and
bags full of things I don't really need.
I'll stumble my way past you, without a second look.
You'll want to dash across the street to carry my bags for me, wipe the
sweat from my brow, and begin every conversation you ended before.
But you won't.
I'll get a text from you, later that day, letting me know that you spotted
me.
And I probably won't respond.
Because I'll never know what to say.
But if I do respond,
all I'll say is
"See you soon."
Because though I can't keep you in my life,
I don't believe in goodbyes.
And hopefully I do see you soon.
Because I'm still the girl you fell in love with at 17.
And I think that we will
always,
always,

always,
find a way back to each other.
At least, that's what I want to believe.
The girl that you fell in love with at 17, knows that you're nothing but a
fragment of her love story.
Maybe she loves you still.
I don't know much about that.
See you soon.

Just to Clarify.

He moaned such a soft
'I love you' into my ear
that I barely caught it.
When I asked him
what he had said,
just to clarify,
he blushed and told me,
he said nothing that time.

Two years later,
after I left him,
he calls me up on the phone,
to finally let me know,
that he did indeed moan an
'I love you' into my ear.

When I ask him
why he never told me earlier,
just to clarify,
he laughs and tells me,
that he was afraid
that I would leave
and deem the
'I love you.'
Worthless.

So I tell him,
if he had just had clarified,
that night,
that he did indeed love me,
he would not have had to call me
2 years later because
I would not have left him.
I left him because I felt
that he was too afraid
to love,

and that if he knew me better,
he would've known,
that I wanted him to moan it again.

And so he asks me,
over the phone,
if I would ever consider trying again.
When I ask him
why he decided to ask now,
just to clarify,
he tells me that he feels safe now.
I inhale and tell him,
that I like danger.
And anyways,
he's 2 years too late.

I whisper such a soft
'I love you' over the phone,
that he barely catches it.
When he asks,
what I had said,
just to clarify,
I giggle and tell him
'I loved you, one time.'

Kind Of.

You can ask if I miss him.
I'll tell you I do.
It's that simple.
But if you asked you how much I missed him,
I'd give you poetry.
Because some days, I miss him like melancholy summer days miss the
adrenaline of pumping out an essay in under an hour.
Some days I miss him with numb fingers and empty pockets.
Some days I miss him without knowing, casually living life while his
memory sleeps between my teeth.
Some days it feels a lot like thunderstorms and imagination, beautiful,
but so dangerous.
Some days I wake up with empty pens and sheets stained with runny
mascara.
He said he'd stay.
He said he'd stay.
I wish he stayed.
Some days I miss him like I miss the pleasant aroma of peaceful
December nights.
Some days I miss him enough to browse our messages and write him
poetry coded with our silly jokes.
Some days I miss him enough to trick myself into believing I need him.
Some days I sleep at 10 pm, happy, because of how right I was to let him
go.
Most days, I'm completely happy.
Most days, I love and live without his essence shutting me down.
Most days, I know, I've gotten over him.
But still,
Some days I miss him enough to write him tornados and cry him floods.
And,
Most days I just miss him like endnotes.
He's just another "yeah, I miss him."
for anyone who asks.

But lately nobody does.

Hopeful.

Someone's going to love me.

Maybe not like the way you loved me on Monday mornings with your rose petal lips leaving blue and black rose buds on my neck.

Maybe not like the way you loved me wordlessly in your almost broken down Toyota with your fingers writing love songs on my thighs.

Maybe not like the way you loved me with a million accents and a million play pretend names to show me that you could indeed love me in a million different ways.

Maybe not like the way you loved me with your own eyes, always undressing my entire being, always overflowing with a concoction of desire and a little splash of love.

And your love was damn amazing.

But someone's going to love me,

Maybe not like you.

But their love is going to be damn fulfilling.

Their love is going to be just what I need.

Not A Love Poem.

This is not a love poem.

When I wake up at four am, a blanket so twisted between my legs that I'm reminded of the vacancy next to me, I'll unravel myself and return to sleep.

When the rain pours so hard that puddles form beneath my feet, I'll throw my hair back and let the rain stream down my face to wash the day away.

When I wake the next morning, unsure of what to wear, I'll pull together an outfit that'll feel like stilettos and a beaming smile.

When I sing songs in the shower, and the water hits the floor just loud enough to cover my tragic high notes, I'll sing songs about loving myself and I'll feel it in my bones.

When my friends ask me how you're doing, and every memory of you revisits to taunt me, I'll wave them away and tell them that you're probably doing okay.

When I dig up those pressed flowers that sat like unopened letters in my closet, I'll release them outside, they don't have a *home* with me any longer.

When I pull out old notebooks with love notes to you scrawled in every corner, I'll laugh and praise myself for the way I was so capable of putting my thoughts into words.

When you text me again in the middle of summer, asking for another chance, I'll have to ask who you are, because I deleted your number so long ago.

When I walk through empty halls with not a single hand to hold, I'll let my graceful hands swing proudly by my hips.

When my body begins to ache for something more, something to release all the tension building within my stomach, I'll go for a run because I may just be getting out of shape.

When some boy that reminds me of you walks up to me to say hello, I'll say hello back to him with a firm handshake and a piercing gaze to keep him away.

When you read this poem, if you ever do, you'll text me to ask why I still write about you with some lingering old love, and I'll laugh and tell you that you completely missed the point, because
This is not a love poem.

Mute.

A year of dropped calls, undelivered text messages, text messages I couldn't bear to write, broken connections and a whole fucking year of silence.

Silence.

Silent as my wavering cries at 4 am when I shoved them straight back down my throat so that I wouldn't wake the neighbors.

Silent as the I love you's that stopped escaping your lips once you'd learned we just weren't a good fit.

Silent as the radio I turned down because our song started playing and I just needed to fucking drive.

Silent as my phone became, no longer bombarded with messages from you, asking if I was doing okay.

Silent as the party noises you started to drown out, searching for my honey toned voice in the crowd.

Silent as my pen gliding across the paper, leaking ink colored with the way you once said my name.

Silent as the midnight, as we both lay awake scrolling through old photographs and messages we swore we wouldn't revisit ever again.

Someone once told me that silence is deafening, that sometimes silence would be the loudest thing you'd ever hear.

But our silence is just quiet.

It's muted by the distance that has grown between us.

No longer do we desire so strongly to put the silence to rest between us.

The silence is comforting. It reminds me that you don't exist quite so loudly anymore.

The silence will live until my choked up cries turn to laughter, until I tell myself to love myself, until I turn the radio up and belt the words to every damn song that comes on, until my mother texts me to ask me if I'm okay, until the party noises get so loud you have to cover your ears and sing along, until my pen runs out of ink and I use a scratchy, old pencil instead, and until we both fall asleep at ten pm with our snores to fill the air.

The silence rips and shreds at our core, it hurts like the hell, but we need it.

The silence will heal us.

So do me one last favor, my dear.

Shh...

First Loves.

Love begins within your core.

You won't notice it until its dainty little fingers start brushing up against your heart.

Even then, you won't know what you're feeling. It just tickles a little, like your insides forgot their regular routines.

Then, just three weeks later, your fingertips are throbbing with a need to create things as beautiful as you feel and your lips are overflowing with the songs of love.

All you want to do is to feel them embrace you, warm you up, remind you that you are okay. Suddenly the world is comfortable, warm and bright.

This is the youngest and freshest love you'll ever feel.

This is the first love.

When your heart feels the touch of another in such a way for the first time, it rages with an engulfing fire. The first love is the one love you can't forget no matter how hard you try.

Sometimes, but only sometimes, love burns with a fire so massive that it sucks away all the oxygen from your lungs and expires with a final burst. Suddenly you're learning how to breathe again, but this time for yourself, not for the fire inside of you.

Your body coils from its inside and rejects every loving touch, afraid that you still haven't learned how to control the inferno.

You learn that you've let hope burn away in the flames and that somewhere along the way, you sacrificed things you need now more than ever.

This is not the end. You have not burnt out and you will find yourself again soon.

Reach inside yourself when you're ready, uncoil your tangled organs and massage them back to life.

It just tickles a little.

It just tickles a little.

Divisions Monologue.

He still loves you.

From the delicate, pink apples of your cheeks to the plump, miniature grapes of your toes.

Open mouthed stares and weary, drifting gazes just won't keep him away.

His heart beats every second for a second chance to have a few more moments with you.

He knows his own wrongdoings, and they twist and turn him until he's writhing in bed, wondering how he can make things right with what he has left.

Every morning he wakes with the taste of your peachy plump lips on the tip of his tongue, your careless signature to remind him of what he has lost.

He still loves you.

He pours his heart out into poetry that he never knew was possible for him to write. Words of anguish and despair cloud the air around his head, and his body aches to just be back in your bed.

His chest feels like a graveyard as your fireworks start to sizzle out and die in his ribcage. A graveyard to host his slow beating heart and big, drowning dreams.

And 3 am.

He still loves you. At 3 fucking am.

You touched his fucking soul and grasped it in your graceful fingers and he was so fucking graceless about how he maneuvered his way through your beautiful, full heart but hell yes he'd do it again, as many times as it took until you realized that he's been in love with you since day motherfucking one and damn, baby your hair looked so beautiful under the moonlight when he took you skinny dipping, and goddamn your words were the most enriching form of song he ever heard and your tiny hands were holding more than just his hands and why the hell did you have to let go, he fucking loves you, he fucking loves you, he fucking loves you, he still fucking loves you at 3 fucking am, 4 am, 24 hours a day and why can't he tell you anymore why the fuck did he let something so beautiful slip through the hands he let you hold, how is love allowed to hurt this bad, why does it hurt so much for him to love you?

80

And at 4 am.
You still love him.
But you bathe in silence with his favorite shirt clinging to the tender skin of your body.
You still love him.
He still loves you.
And you both know it's over. There is no round two. You're slowly drifting away into separate spheres, never to collide in the same way again.
But it's still going to hurt.

It's just different now.
He still loves you.
You still love him.
And it's all okay.
The End.

Fun Animal Facts.

Did you know, cows have four stomachs just to digest the tough food they intake?
Even with four stomachs I still don't believe I'd ever be able to digest every lie I swallowed when I was with you. They've always been too tough, hiding away between my teeth and searching for blood.

Did you know, if you were to put a goldfish in a dark room, that one day it would pale and not be so golden anymore?
And that makes sense, I saw you as the light I needed to live in a world of gold. Romances grow tired after a while, and when October rolled around I realized that you had been keeping me in the dark, hidden within your shadow. Your lips trembled as you watched our romance rust over, and the funny thing is that only fools gold rusts.

Did you know, that many butterflies are rather toxic?
Pretty things have an ugly side, if not treated with caution. I overdosed on the pretty, let myself fly for a while before finally coughing up your broken promises and pretty excuses. And when I was lying there on the ground, peering at the way your lips curved like angel wings, all I could think was: "thank god my body knew just how to get rid of your toxin."

Did you know, a starving mouse will eat its own tail?
I've been told that fantasies are easily swallowed, but don't end up being too fulfilling. I just wanted you to prove me wrong, give me something real to chew on, something to accompany your promises. So I waited, waited, and waited until my stomach cried out for something real. I chose to swallow my tongue then, because it wasn't my place to ask you for anything more. It really was my fault, I expected too much from you.

Did you know, a human is one of the only animals capable of loving so hard that it begins to hurt?
It's true what they say. Love really is blinding. My heart grew so large just to accommodate your soul, and you barely set one foot in. And it is because of that love that I felt the worst pain known to humankind. My heart burst. There was too much empty space within my chest, space that

you couldn't fill. And there was nothing left to do but watch as my wasted love spilled over the sides of my ribcage.

Did you know, tigers are one of the strongest animals on earth? Sorry if you thought that you'd become my last lover. Sorry if you thought I was writing to tell you I'll never move on. I'm quite strong, and you're just another story I'll someday overcome. And please, don't ever try to come back, you are no match for a tiger.

Change.

Things are changing.

I've forgotten your voice, the melancholy sweetness of it and the husky undertones of it.

Things are changing.

I deleted old messages and scrapped old photographs that were collecting dust on my bookshelf.

Things are changing.

I reread my high school diary, dragging my finger across the parts about you, cringing softly at my naivety and desire.

Things are changing.

I closed that diary and tossed it out with my unfinished math homework and B+ essays.

Things are changing.

Most of my stuff is in boxes, crammed up against one another, patiently waiting to be jostled into a new home.

Things are changing.

I think I cry more over sweet elderly dogs finding joy in daffodils and antsy squirrels than I do over you.

Things are changing.

To be completely honest, I never cry over you anymore.

Things are changing.

You've found your passions, I'm seeking out mine, we finally exist in separate spheres living the world on our own.

Things are changing.

I love myself now, more than ever. And it feels like *home*.

Things are changing.

You've grown your hair out, your face grew older and your words speak wiser. I am proud of you. Liberation looks beautiful on you.

Things are changing.

I now finally have an answer to the probing question 'how long does it take to get over someone?'

3 years. It took me 3 years to get over you.

Things have changed.

4. Human Observation.

I've been told that learning about other people teaches you a lot about yourself. Especially when you see bits and pieces of your being in other people and you are able to critically think about who you want to be.

So before finding a place to call home, I observed human nature, who we were, and what we needed to survive. This piece of me isn't just a piece of me, but a piece of other people as well.

This here is a miscellaneous collection of me learning other people and finding my place in the madness.

Pretty Girl.

And she was pretty,
she was.
But she was more than just pretty,
she was.
The word 'pretty' felt inadequate when held up to her.
Her skin was pretty, her hair was pretty, her eyes were astonishingly
pretty, and her words were even more pretty,
but she?
She was so much more than pretty,
she was.
She was the kind of pretty that most minds do not know how to
comprehend.
She was the kind of pretty that people stopped and listened to.
She was the kind of pretty that didn't know how to sit still.
She was the kind of pretty that wasn't simply pretty.
I'd call her beautiful,
but even that seems inadequate.
She was just,
her.
So much more than pretty,
so much more than beautiful,
everything that we know to be spectacular,
compressed together in one pretty little mind.

Artists, Poets.

You fell in love with the artist,
the one who,
even after you broke their heart,
made you look like something
breathtaking,
made you sound like
a miracle.
They wrote you a thousand poems,
crafted you a million different ways,
all allowing you to exist within the lines of
beauty.
Do you know how lucky you are?
To have broken the heart of someone,
someone who will turn you into art?
You've been alive before,
but never like this.

Woman.

Goddess.

They emblazon the word across the voluptuous breasts of a freshly birthed 18 year old.

Goddess.

We let the word slip out lips in a breathless song as we gaze at the dips and curves of a young woman's body.

Goddess.

They tell me, that the word goddess is a title for every woman's body that looks like a woman's body.

Goddess.

But what the hell is a woman's body if it's exclusive to bodies that most women do not have.

Goddess.

What is the worth of a definition that does not fit snugly over the curves (or lack thereof) of all those it defines.

Goddess.

And why are we labeling women based solely on their bodies anyways?

Goddess.

A woman is more than a body, her body does not determine her womanhood. She is a woman if she chooses to be, she is a woman regardless of what she is told to be.

Goddess.

A woman is a mind, ideas bursting from neurons, passion spiraling out in tight curls. A woman is a heart, softly pumping every drop of life she can into the world. A woman is made of words that will never be able to supply an adequate definition. A woman cannot be defined.

Goddess.

Strip the word off of her breasts, and let her take the matter into her own hands.

Goddess.

A woman is a goddess, though the word may never do her justice. She can choose the words she wants to hold to her name.

Woman.

She is her own.

Poets vs. Bullies.

Make people cry from the beauty of your words
rather than the cruelty of your words.
Remind them that they can feel.
Remind them that feeling doesn't always feel like falling apart.

Graduation 2016.

And 13 years later,
it has ended.
Another era becoming history,
another moment becoming
unforgettable.
When we scan the rows of bright, shiny smiles,
we remember the days we felt like this chapter was never going to end.
All of us, together, holding our breath for that final
'congratulations, you made it.'
Our feet ache from standing,
our lips are numb from speaking,
but we are filled with the energy of a million suns,
ready to
explode.
A tear escapes from some of our eyes,
reminding us that though we are about
to embark on something new,
this is all we've ever known,
and leaving this behind is the strangest change we will overcome.

And to all of us who never knew we'd make it,
to all of us that got lost along the way,
to all of us who didn't achieve every one of our goals,
and
to all of us who continued to get back up every single time,
we are here together.
We are about to get another chance.

This is a beginning, not an end.
So our fingers wiggle in anticipation
just before those words are spoken.
'Congratulations, class of 2016, you made it!'
Cheers erupt from every corner of the massive auditorium,
caps fly,
and we all let out a collective sigh.
And it's over.
Just like that.
Congratulations, class of 2016.
You've made it,
we've made it.
Now let's get on with the rest
of our lives.

Humbled.

There is a girl who lives
On the tips of
Stars
And she dances with the sharp edges
Tickling her feet
Her hair is soaked in
Stardust
Her body lives in eternal
Paradise
But one day, the girl starts to
Question
All she has ever known
So she spies the smaller people
Living
On the blue and green planet
It doesn't look like what she
Feels
So she
Jumps
Straight down through sky
Straight down to the sphere
She sees people pointing in awe
Calling her a shooting
Star
So she pirouettes past clouds
And watches her star light
Disappear
Until she looks just like the
Rest
She greets the ground with a heartfelt
Thump
When she sees the inquiring
Faces
She giggles a small little giggle and
Speaks
Pleasure to meet you, pleasure indeed.

It isn't quite as lonely down here.
It feels a lot like
Home.

Life Enamors Me.

I think it's quite odd how the simplest questions can bring back complicated memories, and then go unanswered.

I think it's ridiculous how people can just stop talking and simply forget they ever did.

I find it strange how we find metaphors in blowing blades of grass and winding gravel paths.

I think it's absolutely wondrous how we all fall asleep and dream about things we can't even imagine awake.

I think it's absolutely terrifying that we can fall in love and fall apart so quickly.

I think it's truly beautiful that we all die insignificant to the universe, but completely significant to somebody.

Lost.

she laid still in the grass,
it was nearing midnight and a chilly fog hung in the air above her.
hours before, she had lost
everything.
but she never cried,
never blubbered incoherent words of remorse.
instead she took a walk outside,
sunk into a grassy field
and just laid there,
motionless.

so when i saw her,
i asked her,
'what's keeping you from feeling?'
there was a moment of heavy silence
before
her soft chuckles drifted from her lips,
'i knew this would happen.' she whispered,
'nothing ever goes right.
i've been preparing to lose
everything
since day one.
it's just so much easier to forget

that happy endings exist.'
so i sunk into the grass as well,
the somber mood washing over me.
'what a clever trick,' i thought to myself.
but it really wasn't a clever trick,
not one at all.
but i kept my sobs muted
and together we mourned the loss
of her once vivid hope.

Commitment.

He said to me:

'You quit piano, you quit soccer, you quit gymnastics, and you quit basketball. You can't blame me for being afraid to commit to someone who knows how to quit.'

And I said to him:

'Piano, soccer, gymnastics and basketball were simply hobbies. So if you thought that our relationship would be just a hobby, then you don't truly know what a commitment is.'

More Than.

Quite frankly,
she was art.
We loved her,
we loved looking at her.
But she didn't enjoy herself
as much.
She didn't love seeing herself
as much.
Because to her,
she was nothing extraordinary.
And we told her,
we told her every day,
that she was beautiful,
that she rivaled the most
exquisite art.
And she laughed in our faces,
a beautiful laugh at that.
And within a few months,
we watched her drift into the skies,
her beauty disappearing beyond
the clouds.

'She was so beautiful'

we said.
But when she finally reached
the stars,
she looked down upon us,
smiled weakly,
and simply whispered:
'I wish I was more than just
beautiful.
I wish they knew my
substance.

I wish they saw words
and not just skin.'
and quite frankly,
she was art.
She was just tired
of people
finding art in
the way her voice
sounded,
rather than finding
art
in what her voice
could do.
But gee,
wasn't she beautiful?

Thank Goodness You're Gone.

It's okay to be happy when people leave.
Because sometimes a person's presence is a prison of its own.
Sometimes you cannot leave until they do.
So do not feel guilty when you feel a spark of gratitude at their absence.
Instead, remember that you never needed them,
Let that 'thank you' slip from your lips,
And don't forget to shut the doors behind you.

The Girl.

she was in love with everything,
and it was so damn contagious.
we found ourselves all falling in love with her,
lips gaping, eyes bright and sparkly.
she swayed and sashayed in the wind,
making love to the ground beneath her.
and all we could do was watch,
enamored by the way she made us feel like poetry.
decades later, we heard that she'd passed.
we showed up to her funeral, dressed in feathery black, seeking
something to hold onto.
soft wind cruised through our skirts, tugging our bodies into a breezy
dance.
so with our lips gaping, eyes bright and sparkly with tears,
we came together once again,
falling in love
the way we knew
she would want us to.

28 Years.

And then he said,
'Maybe it's okay.
Maybe, it was supposed to go this way.
Maybe we're going to break,
but I think I'll be okay.
It's okay to let it end,
endings are the beginning of growth.
Yeah, I'll be okay.'
And it was okay,
it always was.
Life was turbulent and that would never change,
but nothing was hopeless.
It took him 28 years to realize this.

Antidote.

Realize this: There are people in your life who are poison.
They are only there to break you down, intoxicate you and leave you shaken.
Realize this: You are the only antidote.
You can say goodbye, flush them out and begin to build yourself up again.

Healing.

I think that one day, in the near future, you'll be walking through a quaint little grocery store. You'll be picking out the tomatoes that aren't too ripe to be eaten tomorrow, when you start to realize that there's something new that coexists with your essence.

That's when you'll drop the firm tomato into the plastic bag and realize how little you feel the pain you felt waking up for the past few months. You'll have an aura of peace and you'll feel that your life has finally begun to become the type of art you only ever dreamt of before.

Because though you don't know it now, things grew to be better.

You won't feel it change, nobody ever really does.

But it will.

And you'll leave the quaint little store with exactly what you came for.

5. Human Reminders.

Whilst observing the struggles of other people alongside my own, I crafted many reminders and thoughts for us all to live by.

We deserve to value ourselves and our lives to the fullest, but many times we are limited by our own self-doubt and reservations.

In my journey to find my home, I figured that writing these poems could help guide me down the right path as well, so these are the many poems I wrote hoping that if I could just live by my own words,

Maybe I'd come home.

Soon.

You're going to feel this life
growing gradually underneath your tongue.
Swelling up like a ripe cherry,
softer and softer till the tender skin bursts.
And then you'll taste it,
the sweetest taste to ever stain your teeth.
Deep, maroon cherry juices dribbling down your chin,
slick, shiny, bloody looking.
Soon.
You're going to feel this life
and when you do,
you will understand that you exist.
You
exist.
Your life will come alive,
and you will feel it,
soon.

Free.

You see,
that's the hard part about living.
Everything has an end.
It's just that some endings take so long to get to,
that it feels like forever.
But, you see,
that's also the easy part about living.
Everything has an end.
So one day,
you'll realize that forever
was not really forever.
And that will be a blessing,
not a curse.

Do Not Forget.

we are told
that we are made of
stardust.
that we are nothing
but a million mistakes
all happening in perfect
time,
just to let us exist.
we are created from
broken dreams
supernovas
first breaths
and last steps.
and it's
such a small chance,
unthinkably small,
that you'd be sitting where
you are now-
reading this,
contemplating existence,
and yet you are.
there were ten trillion
mistakes
that led up to this
very
moment.
you
are not one
of them.
your very existence
is far rarer
than winning the lottery,
getting mauled by a bear,
and getting swept away by a tornado
all in the same day.

you are rare,
exquisite,
made up of stardust
and impossible connections.
let that be a reminder
to the profound meaning
of your
ever growing life.

Bandage.

You love calling people your "bandages," preaching about how gently they healed you.

However, what you haven't realized is how bandages merely shelter your wounds.

A bandage never truly heals anything, it only stands guard as your body does the healing on its own.

Just remember that the next time you call someone your "bandage."

You do the healing on your own.

It is not the bandage that knows how to craft new skin and ease your pain,

that's all you.

It's your body that fought off danger with a dazzling display.

It's your body that learned how to heal.

So yes, that person may have been your bandage,

but they did not fix you.

You fixed you.

Understand that.

Living.

exist, love, dream, live.
forget that you are constrained by time,
live so wholly you forget time exists.
you will never be younger,
you will never have more life brimming inside of you.
so,
why are you wasting yourself on things you do not love,
on places you do not come alive in,
on people who do not make you better.
be selfish and take advantage of yourself.
now is not the time to sit back and wait.
live.
live.
live.
live until you become your own universe.
just live.
in whatever way,
just don't forget to live.

The Most Poetic Thing.

Someone once told me
that poetry could exist without words.
And though I didn't believe them for a while,
I finally discovered poetry within myself.
Poetry existed in the way I came from dandelions, but lived in the city of roses.
and,
poetry existed in the way I made the city my own.
Poetry existed in the way I danced on the brink of freedom every day,
believing that the world could soon be mine.
Poetry existed in the way I watched every sunset with a dash of childlike
wonder, capturing every second as the sun melted into the earth.
Poetry existed in my passion, the way that I always devoted myself
completely to everything I loved.
Poetry existed in the way that I let myself grow, understanding that my
failures would only be failures if I could not learn from them.
And most of all,
poetry existed in the mere way I lived within the universe.
You see,
I am a human who is constantly changing, developing and becoming.
Just look how far I have come.
Because that's poetry.
And for me,
tomorrow is just another sunrise and 86,400 seconds of raw possibility.
Tomorrow is just another chance to make my life come alive.

Someone once told me
that poetry could exist without words.
and I hope you believe me
when I say,
that you too are the epitome of poetry.
You have a chance in this world.
It's about time that you just
take it.
Because
there's something strangely poetic about a life well lived.

Human.

It's thrilling
to feel so much, all at once.
It's as if you were exploding
and coming back to life
at the same time.
You're falling apart,
but at least you know
you're human.

Almosts.

He liked the way she looked,
like sea glass, almost too beautiful to touch.
almost.
He had this brutal way about him, and I always saw him in the color
maroon. It was almost hard to fall in love with him.
almost.
She flew past clouds at four am, delving into her own small existence,
feeling the weights spill from her soul. She almost found herself.
almost.
She promised herself that she'd try her hand at commitments, so she
told him that she'd be around past noon. She almost stayed.
almost.
The cancer slivered through his brain, and we lost him before he ever
left his body. We almost got in a goodbye.
almost.
She spent days shuffling through the broken glass on the pavement,
scraping her knees and cutting her fingers. She almost found her beauty.
almost.
He realized that he was numb when he had to touch it all in order to feel
anything. So he grasped my palms to feel my pulse, and he almost felt my
love.
almost.
At 4:54 pm on Saturday evening, he decided that he didn't want to live
anymore. He almost changed his mind.
almost.

almost.
almost says 'maybe next time.'
almost says 'guess it won't work out like that.'
almost says 'guess it won't work out.'
almost says 'you had your shot. you messed it up.'
almost says 'fuck you.'
almost says 'why couldn't you save him?'
almost says 'you lost it.'
almost says 'it was never supposed to be.
almost says 'if you had just been there at 4:30 pm...'
almost screams your name the shrillest at 1:22 am when you've almost
forgotten it all.
almost.
but when you *almost* give up,
don't.

Daughter.

Baby girl, you are beautiful.

Your existence brings joy to me every day, from the way you speak to the way you smile, you have always been the epitome of beauty and you always will be.

Baby girl, growing up is tough.

The bullies will laugh your stomach out of the room, and your heart will drop just to fill the empty space inside. Look past that, please. Forget that their words ever meant to matter.

Baby girl, you're going to feel different.

The world is going to seem so perfectly aligned all the time, and goddamn if you could be too, you would be too. Your mind is the darkest monster you're going to battle, but sometimes it's okay to tell it to just shut the fuck up.

Baby girl, there will be days when you can't bear anything.

Your crying will turn to an overwhelming sense of numbness, and your head will pound. You'll question your existence in every possible way and wonder if you're worth the life you've been given. You are. You're worth every second.

Baby girl, you'll feel alone.

You'll lie awake at night with a pen in hand, scribbling out love letters that you don't ever address. Stop searching for love, it comes for you.

Baby girl, friends can be mean too.

You don't need to compromise yourself all the time to satisfy the needs of others. You are an independent woman, act like it.

Baby girl, being 13 doesn't equate to maturity.

There is no need to prove yourself with drugs, sex or anything that the world tells you to get dressed for. Do not be hasty, and grow up at your own pace.

Baby girl, don't be petty.

I know the kids around you bask in gossip, lies and hateful words I hope you never speak, but you'll be so much happier when you can treat every person you meet with a degree of respect. That is maturity.

Baby girl, study hard.

Middle school, high school, I know it's a drive down into hell, but make the best of it. Don't get caught up in that boy who doesn't like you back, or the girl who exists only to hurt you. Remember that none of this will matter once you've achieved success.

Baby girl, you're going to be so confused.

You'll spend so many days wondering who you really are, what you want and where you're going. Don't worry about figuring it all out just yet. You'll grow into yourself eventually, don't force it.

Baby girl, you're going to feel heartbreak.

Heartbreak lasts a long time, and it leaves you with some scars and a need to write angsty poetry to drive it all away. But it doesn't last forever, so don't pretend that it will. Go out and live.

Baby girl, don't let grades or test scores define you.

Whether you score poorly or score extremely well, the only thing that should define you, is you. Congratulate yourself when you do well, but always recognize the room for improvement.

Baby girl, be confident.

Wear confidence like a stamp, display it with pride. Love yourself and who you are. You might not know it yet, but your confidence is what's going to bring the world to your feet. Let it grow on you, fake it until you make it.

Baby girl, nothing matters more than your happiness.

Remind yourself of this every day. Do the things that make you happy. Your main goal in life should be to achieve happiness, won't matter if you achieve this by becoming an artist or going to medical school so long as you are happy.

Baby girl, stand up for yourself.

Stand up until your legs hurt. Make your voice heard, and don't let an injustice pass through your ears if it makes you cringe.

Baby girl, you are beautiful.

My goodness, if you haven't figured this out by now, you are so beautiful. You're going to grow up so much in these next few years, but don't forget that you're beautiful. You may not feel it right now, but you will.

Baby girl, you are beautiful.

Let that sink in.

Someday, My Dear.

Someday you're going to be sitting in a little loft above the New York
City sky
and you're going to watch people stumbling over cracks in the road,
alongside frantic tourists getting lost.
You'll recognize yourself in the sadness of some of the passerby,
but you're going to be happy.
You're going to be okay.
And you're going to know that your life is just beginning.

6. Me.

I have taken you through the love I've faced, the loss I've faced, the healing I've done and the people I've watched go through the same things. But I haven't yet taken you through me, just me. Raw, uninhibited me.

And I don't mean to sound like I'm some unique flower amongst it all, so I hope that you can find pieces of yourself in this chapter as well.

This chapter will contain the parts of me that festered up while I was on my road to self-discovery. This is me without a true home. This is me before I came to really be *me*.

Ignorance.

there's a lot of things i don't know.
for example,
i don't know today,
i don't know tomorrow.
i don't know if my life is good,
or just mediocre.
i don't know if i'm any good,
or if i'm just mediocre.
i don't know if i'm happy,
or just too distracted to see i'm not.
i don't know if i can solve my problems,
i don't know if my problems need solving.
i don't know who i should love,
or who i'm supposed to regret.
i don't know if my good memories are real,
or simply embellishments of nothing special.
i don't know if we will exist in 10 years,
but i don't know if i really care.
i don't know if i'm bored,
or just too caught up in the same old routine.
i don't know
if i want to know
all the things i don't know.
i just don't know.
i only want to exist
so vividly
that it won't matter
that i know nothing,
or that nothing knows me
all that well.
i just want to know myself,
a little bit.
just a little, tiny bit.

Faces of Okay.

I'm okay: I'm okay.

I'm okay: I'm doing better than I was yesterday.

I'm okay: I can breathe right today.

I'm okay: I love the way the stars look right now, I'm glad I'm here.

I'm okay: Thank you.

I'm okay: I've been hanging on, not doing too badly.

I'm okay: I don't know how else to answer you.

I'm okay: I don't think you'd want to know.

I'm okay: I'm numb right now, I guess that means I'm okay.

I'm okay: I'm doing worse than I was yesterday, but it's not that bad yet.

I'm okay: I forgot how to breathe.

I'm okay: Even if the stars aligned I don't think I'd know what 'okay' felt like.

I'm okay: I've been hanging on to whatever's left.

I'm okay: Please don't remind how I'm feeling.

I'm okay: Talk about yourself. I want to exist as you for a moment.

I'm okay: I wish I wasn't so vulnerable.

I'm okay: I'm not okay.

Tell Me Again.

Tell me again, that it's going to get better.

I'm living in a house with blacked out windows and there you are, trying to wash away the darkness with two drops of water.

Tell me again, that you understand.

I'm locked inside my goddamn house and you're banging down doors telling me that you can see through my blacked out windows.

Tell me again, that you're sorry.

I'm gazing at this house I've created, this house I've locked myself in, this house that has no way out, and you're whispering through the cracks like it's your fault.

Tell me again, that everyone's going to miss me.

I've been locked away for so long. I've been missing for all this time already, stuck in this cold house, and they never even noticed I was already gone.

But really, tell me again.

Because it's comforting to know that there's something potentially beautiful outside my isolated, ugly house.

Artist.

sometimes I enjoy being an artist,
creating things at four am,
unhappy, but not completely sad.
hanging up my work for the world to see,
taking in their curious eyes and pursed lips.
see, I let them figure out what I've created,
craft me a personality based on what they see.
I'd rather them decide who I am than me,
I barely know myself that well anyways.

Happiness Eludes Me.

Beyond anything, happiness eludes me.

It dashes beyond colorful sunsets and vacant, native forests.

It lingers at my own acceptance, demanding I bring someone else to achieve it for me.

Happiness challenges me to find it on my own, but knows I still cannot.

The moment I let happiness slip through my fingers at the age of 12, it decided that it would make me pay for letting it go.

How selfish of me to not have held on tighter.

Muse.

I need a muse,
will you be my muse?
Will you be the words I
write,
hoping one day you'll read them
over my shoulder,
tears welling up beneath your
eyelids.
Saying,
"Baby, I never knew you loved me that much."
Will you be my muse?
All you have to do is exist.
Just make me feel,
feel like every bone in my body
has softened,
like buttery caramel in your
warm palm.
All you have to do is break my heart,
maybe once, twice, ten times.

Or you could love me.
But nobody seems to enjoy that.
Make me feel.
Make me feel.
Be my muse,
please.
Give me something to say.
I need a muse.
Say you'll be my muse.
Tell me you'll stay.

Mediocrity.

Everything around me was at rest.
Not a single word spoken,
not a single breath taken.
My fingers clutched my own thighs,
cursing my existence.
I said,
I'm living because I haven't had the blessing of death yet.
Mediocrity is unfortunate.
I'd rather be the world's best dirt eater,
than the world's most mediocre.
If I kissed another set of lips tonight,
how good would I feel?
Would it feel like plump cherries on the Fourth of July?
Or fireworks fizzing and forgetting to die?
I said,
sorry for expecting a universe when I can only live in a world.
A world that I wish I owned,
when the most I'll ever own
is a home.
Mediocrity is unfortunate.
I'd rather be something strange,
than something forgettable.
Everything grew louder then.
So many words spoken that I couldn't understand a single one.
I couldn't breathe.
Of course,
I was never the only one.
Mediocrity is unfortunate.
I said,
I am nothing.
I am not okay with it,
but I have to learn to be.
I said,
expect nothing,
you'll be satisfied when anything comes around.
Mediocrity is unfortunate,
and that is okay.

Unfinished Business.

I am a woman of unfinished business.
Unfinished paintings hanging on my walls, unfinished poetry idling in my drafts, unfinished tv seasons haunting me.

I am a woman of unfinished business.

That painting is almost done, I just haven't finished the background. I'm afraid that I'll fuck it up, and that whatever if envisioned for the painting won't be a reality. I can't stand the thought of finishing art that isn't as beautiful as it was in my head. So I'll leave it blank, to pretend that if I'd ever stepped back into painting, maybe it would've turned out okay.

The poems sit in my drafts, giving me inspiration on a daily basis, reminding me that once I was able to spill poetry like nobodies business. Now those poems just trickle, barely there, fragments of the poet I used to be. I don't want to finish those poems, when I know I'm not capable of giving them the ending they deserve. I'm not done with them yet.

I never watched the last episode of my favorite tv show, one that I watched for 5 years. Instead, I rewatched old seasons and pretended like it wasn't already over. It's been over for 2 years now, and I still haven't watched that last episode. Watching it means closure, it means that there isn't one more episode left, it means that it's time to let go. A tv show episode, such a simple conflict. Yet I still can't garner the heart to let it go.
Most people need closure,
Most people need to let things go,
Frankly, I do too,
but what I need most is,

Nonsensical Meanderings.

ok for two days
not ok for two days
ok for two days
my goodness, i love the way it is.
not ok.
most definitely not ok.
change.
change.
oh you won't change.
i like pink roses when i feel like daffodils.
i am a daffodil when i see pink roses.
is there anything bad about daffodils?
no. there isn't.
ok for two days.
ok for two days.
ok till ok isn't enough.
not ok.
not ok.
fuck pink roses.

Change.
tell me that change isn't sad.
tell me that even when you leave for something better,
a part of you doesn't ache.

because i could be pulled from the depths of hell,
embraced by angel's wings and pillowy clouds,
and a part of me would still break,
a part of me would still wonder what hell felt like
without me in it.

i am the woman who
can't handle any change.
i am the woman who
is afraid that every 'it's about to get better'
is a facade.

and if i had it my way,
i would still be a baby atom
floating perpetually through
one galaxy
never to know change,
never to need it.

How Quickly My Love Recedes.

i was convinced that i loved him,
until i met you.
and i was convinced that i loved you
until i met someone new.
then i was convinced that i loved me,
and gee how that set me free.
but i was only convinced that i loved me,
until i met him.
and now it's glass shards on a gravel floor,
me learning to love me again.

Paintings Within My Stomach.

I feel caged within my body.
As if my soul is brimming over the edges,
diligently waiting to spill over.
I crave an explosion,
one of my own.
My insides bursting from my chest and taking over the sky.
Telling me that I am indeed larger than life,
that everything that I am exists in much more than a small body.
Tell me I'm selfish, tell me I'm conceited,
but I swear,
there's more to me than this.

Validation.

There was a painting that hung on the wall,
splattered with dull grays and modest browns.
It had been a few years since that painting had been hung up,
waiting for a pair of wandering eyes.
But that painting never caught a glimpse of life, at least, not then.
That room remained perpetually empty, but that painting was art
nonetheless.
So it hung,
patiently waiting for the soul that that was intrigued enough by the dull
grays and modest browns
to look beyond the fading lines.

Thank You.

I think the reason I miss the people in my life who hurt me,
is because they were the ones who made me stronger.
They helped me learn how to fight for myself.
They helped me realize that I am my own ally.
And somewhere along those lines, I learned to harness my pain,
and turn it into art.

Independence.

I might be an easy person to let go of.

My arms are slippery with the sweat and blood of those who tried to hold on to me in the past, so don't be surprised when your hands slide off my fingertips and clutch empty air.

It's hard to hold on to a free bird, one that has always been somewhat defiant.

Though I'm sure it looks beautiful from down below,

to be able to roam the world with such ease that the clouds become a bed, my spirit is not for you to latch onto.

I live exceptionally, and I do it on my own.

If you have nothing to offer but a desire to dig your nails into my skin solely to taste the sun, know that I will throw you off.

I don't need someone to complete me, and I have no desire to fill voids that will only drag me under.

My spirit simply wants someone to share her world with, she does not need to share herself.

So come, join me if you wish, in the world I've created for myself out of the hope and passion that was born from my chest.

We can be together, so long as you don't try to use me as a free ride into the stars.

Think of me as a companion, rather than a conquest, and we will get along just fine.

I live on the edge of something so profound that my mind has yet to visualize it.

Come along with me,

Become a part of this,

And we may just become a part of something

Incomprehensible.

Bringing Beauty.

And that was the day I stopped calling myself ugly.

I decided that if I couldn't find a speck of beauty waltzing on my eyelids or cartwheeling across my cheeks, then I'd have to dig it out from the fires billowing within my chest.

And that was when I found that the beauty that existed most passionately within me was not the beauty of my physical being, but the beauty of my aging soul.

The beauty I have brought into this world may not be something I can see in many mirrors, because the beauty I have brought into this world comes in the form of art and words.

7. Self-Love.

And here it is, the conclusion to my collection. After years and years of searching for a home, I finally found one in myself.

The beautiful thing about self-love is that it transforms people. It crafts a whole new outlook on life and opens all the doors you assumed were locked.

All through my teen years, I never once thought "maybe I should just love myself instead of seeking other people to do it for me." Well now I am 18, and not only do I love myself, but I know who it is I'm loving.

It's euphoric to have finally made it home.

Fake it Till You Make it.

I'm going to love myself so good that I forget your name.

I'm going to start breathing the air outside, instead of claiming you to be my poetic, bullshit "oxygen."

I'm going to create my own music playlists, ones that fill me with joy instead of dusty memories.

I'm going to banter so often that I realize that you really are not the only person who can make me feel that way.

I'm going to write poetry like this every night, just so that I realize that you aren't in my veins like every other poet says,

you aren't my fucking oxygen- I'm alive just fine without you,

you aren't my heartbeat, you aren't my only, you aren't my whole goddamn past, you aren't some fucking song I'll never forget,

you aren't some beautiful, infinitely poetic piece of art that I'll never unsee, you aren't a cigarette that burned out, you aren't a ghost living in my ribcage.

Baby I know I've written miles of poetry that made you sound like priceless art on the walls, but all of it was just to make us seem romantically cliché.

You're just you. Another boy who happened to play with my heart a little. You sure as hell didn't 'break it' as much as I like to say you did.

I was told that the way to move on was to love someone new.

I learned that I could learn to love myself instead of you.

And boom. No more you.

The Romance of Self-Love.

Let's romanticize self-love.

Too often we mislabel self-love for narcissism and cockiness.

Self-love is a mixture of pride and acceptance, and there's nothing distasteful about that.

Too often we let another human's self-love stir up jealousy in our stomachs.

Self-love is achievable for everyone, no matter how regularly we fail to recognize our own beauty.

Self-love is beautiful love, self-love is healthy love and self-love is powerful love.

Let's romanticize self-love.

Because self-love is the one thing that isn't romanticized enough.

Target.

you grew up with a target dwelling on your forehead,
always wondering why the kids snickered behind your back,
always wondering what you ever did do to them.
so when you one day looked in the mirror and caught glimpse of the
obnoxious little target,
a part of you felt glum.
a part of you thought, "gee, i'd make fun of me too."
and truthfully,
that target was never a pretty sight,
nobody understood it,
not even you.
but
you grew up with a target dwelling on your forehead,
and that target was never a pretty sight,
at least,
until you made it so.
and then,
that target was the prettiest damn thing
anyone ever did see.

Compliment Me.

I don't desire compliments based on my physical appearance. I crave
compliments that are directed at the way I carry myself, the way I live,
the way I am.
I want to be complimented on the things that I have made my own.

Tell me that my words weave webs that you could spend years trapped
in.
Tell me that my heart is the grandest organ you've ever experienced.
Tell me that my mind gives you chills when you've tried so hard to stay
warm.
Tell me that I motivate you, that I inspire you, that every part of me
challenges you to be better.
Tell me that my confidence could carry me all the way to the
luminescent moon.
Tell me that I'm the type of human that feels fulfilling.
Tell me that I make you crave a chance to live life.
Tell me that you could imagine yourself spending late nights in ancient
forests with me.
Tell me that you see me becoming something great.

But don't you dare,
don't you ever,
assume that calling me 'beautiful' will bring me to my knees.
I know I'm beautiful,
So, are you going to tell me something I don't know?

Tips to Combat Sadness.

1. Cry. Go on, cry. You deserve it. Every tear you're holding back is just a problem you're not letting go. Let go.

2. Create. Pull out your trusty pencils, your dusty guitar or the crusty paint you bought back in eighth grade. Don't filter yourself, just express yourself. Make it ugly, make it messy, make it raw.

3. Put on your favorite music. Let yourself connect to feelings you can't put into words. Close your eyes, take it in, and let your thoughts dance beneath your eyelids.

4. Call a friend up. Don't be alone all the time. Let yourself melt into your best friend's shoulder, let them tell you it's going to be okay. Maybe it's not okay now, but it's going to be okay.

5. Watch videos of sweet baby animals stumbling over their own feet. It's nice to know that the whole world isn't all bad.

6. Treat yourself. Take yourself out to your favorite restaurant, soak in a steaming bath, remind yourself that it's not impossible to feel okay. You're going to feel okay soon.

7. Converse with yourself, ask yourself questions, try to figure out what's hurting you most. Learn something about yourself. Grow.

8. Recognize that it's okay to be sad for a while. But please don't let the sadness consume you. Know that you're not alone. Right now is the perfect time to be kind to yourself.

Disorganized Self-Love Poem.

love yourself so good you don't need anybody else.
let your self-love be everyone else's relationship goal.
romanticize self-love again.
learn to be whole on your own.
prioritize you.
write yourself a love poem.
massage yourself back together.
you are not broken, you are just forgetting that your skin will heal.
you are not broken, your heart just got lost on the way.
you are not broken, your heart will come back home.
you could be loving yourself right now.

Rebirth.

The moment that he told me:

"I love you."

My heart cracked in half, and butterflies emerged from every maroon crevice.

My lips glistened with joy, and my fingers quivered with electric excitement.

Suddenly, I was lovable.

After a decade of self-loathing, he made me lovable.

So when he left, I stood alone with the rain drenching my shoulders.

My heart cracked open again, and nothing but dust bunnies spilled over the edges.

And it was in that moment, that I finally told myself:

"I love you."

"I love you."

"I fucking love you."

I'd always been a woman searching for love.

However, the love I needed did not lay in the hands of that boy.

Instead, the love I needed most was my own.

It was always right there.

Always.

I just never knew how to

grab it.

On Physical Beauty.

Society puts too much emphasis on physical beauty.

And this, we all know.

But when I tell a girl that she's beautiful, and she laughs as if it's a joke,
I have to wonder.

Or when I tell a boy that his smile is glorious, and the first thing to slip
his mouth is

"Kids used to make fun of my teeth, you know? I don't like my smile
much."

I can't help but be concerned.

Because I see myself in them.

I don't fully believe anyone who tells me I'm beautiful,
immediately I search for an ulterior motive.

And whenever I'm complimented, I remember each and every hateful
word that once hung on my shoulders.

It's only when someone compliments something other than my physical
beauty that I embrace it.

So when I tell the boy that he is unimaginably intelligent,
he blushes, and takes it bashfully.

When I tell the girl that her words move mountains,
she grins and thanks me with pride.

Society has put so much emphasis on physical beauty,
that it has caused us to deny our own.

Your physical beauty exists.

And it is much more than what you have been trained to see.

Falling in Love Without Romance.

Whenever I am asked by someone whether I've ever been in love with a lover,
I always tell them no.
Though I've loved many people and experienced the thrills of young love,
I've never been in love, not really.
Yet I suppose that's not the complete truth.
I suppose I've been in love with other things.
Not in the romantic sort of way though.
It's more like wonder to me.
I've fallen in love with gasping waterfalls, pounding the ground with a thunderous call. I've fallen in love with treetops, swaying back and forth in the breeze, stretching out as the sun beams down on them. I've fallen in love with another poet's poetry, feeling my heart stop when I realize how much of myself I see in their words. I've fallen in love with the pouring rain as it lulls me to sleep with a constant murmur.
But most importantly,

I've fallen in love with myself.

Hell.

one of the biggest manifestations of hell we face in our living lives is the
hell we face when we are at odds with ourselves,
uncomfortable in our bodies,
and at loss with our minds.
once we settle into our skin and make our own selves home,
well it's *home* now,
not hell.

The Art of Living.

I wear my humanity like a gown.
Every day I swallow my pride for breakfast and dance with my eyes shut
and fingers spread wide.
There is beauty in the way my misery ties itself up in a ribbon around my
waist.
There is glory in the way my joy dips to my neckline, all covered in lace.
My hair caresses my neck and whispers sweet nothings into my ear,
urging me to float across the room with more kindness and grace.
My humanity relishes every second that it gets to dance with me.
My very first goodbye sits on the sleeve of my gown, stitched in with
shaky hands and mismatched thread.
My very first love lies at the lower hemlines, tripped over when I forget
to hold it up. I've been falling again and again and again.
Something about the way the skirt falls so subtly over my hips reminds
me that my body dips and swells like waves on a shore.
I feel like art.
Growing up I wore a simple sack dress, I was told that what was inside
me needed to be imprisoned within me.
My body was too small a cage for the life that thrived within me.
So I parted my lips, and let every piece of my humanity spill out onto
me, grow off of me and decorate me until I wore a gown more exquisite
than any I've ever worn.
I became the flawed masterpiece I always knew I was on the inside.
I am human, and I was always told that it would be much more prideful
to pretend that I wasn't.
So every morning, I swallow my pride for breakfast.
And every morning I invite my soul to experience life with me.
My humanity is a gown.
I am human.
And I dance.
Oh how I dance.

Beauty.

She convinced the world that she was beautiful,
yet still did not believe in her beauty.
But when she convinced herself of her own beauty,
she became beautiful,
and the world's opinion did not matter.

Freedom of Self.

A kiss on the lips, gentle, with a breathy exhale that slides newfound intelligence onto my tongue. It plants itself there, awaiting the moment it can blossom into something profound, something that I can transform into words.

The whispers in my ear become insistent that I drop the chains I've so dutifully wrapped around my wrists. They moan and moan at me to listen to myself speak for once.

It becomes a touch, to my skin, fingers lingering at my stomach, trying to feel if I have swallowed everything my tormentors have fed me. And those fingers delve deeper, to pull those things from my stomach and burn them.

Those are my fingers, I think.

Graceful hands slip a blindfold off of my eyes with a soft touch, but they leave it on the bridge of my nose, still obscuring my line of sight.

I didn't even know that I was blind.

And my hands work. They work to free themselves of the chains I so dutifully trapped myself under. They writhe in anguish till the chains are stained with red and anger splatters the insides of my eyelids. And so they pull, one last time, in final frustration.

The chains have broken.

I throw the blindfold to the floor and see myself for the first time.

My body looks like a battlefield, and my heart beats with the pops of gunshots.

There are flowers growing through my lips, and new life seems pulses its way through my blood, all to remind me that I am here. I am alive.

And it's still eerie to me, because I never knew that I had ever stopped living my life.

Radiance.

A woman can be beautiful,
with skin soft like cotton candy,
or jagged spikes erupting at her wrist.
A woman can be beautiful,
with words sweet like rich chocolate,
or raw like dripping honey.
A woman can be beautiful,
with her body swelling and dipping like the ocean,
or smooth and still like a frozen pond.
A woman can be beautiful,
in any way, in any form
because a woman's radiance is beauty.
And there is no greater radiance
than a that of a woman who has finally learned
self-love.

18.

and now you're 18,
the age which you swore you'd be okay by.
at 17 you started to doubt if you'd ever be okay,
but surprisingly, you are okay.
you never saw it coming either.
you were laying in bed, twisted up in sheets, quietly realizing that it had
been ages since you last cried yourself to sleep.
and you're wondering why you let all those little things hurt you when
you were 14, wondering why you let people take advantage of you at 15,
wondering why on earth you never expected to survive another year at
16.
and it's not that you're never sad anymore,
it's just that you're no longer consumed by your own sadness.
and you're 18 now,
worse things have happened than bad breakups and frizzy hair,
mama cries more often and prays for a gentler hand on your family.
so for the first time,
you've become a rock, making light of the worst situations.
at 18, you always expected to be okay,
running through fields of flowers,
grown up, beautiful, everything laid out for you, making all the right
decisions and loving all the right people, all with a perpetual grin on
your face.
and nothing's like that,
you're confused, lost, unsure, carrying the weight of your own potential
on your aching shoulders, you still don't have your life laid out, and you
still cry about the little things.
but for the first time in your life
you're okay.
you're truly okay.

The Beginning.